THE MISTAKES THAT MADE ME

Part 01

ROHIT RAJU JETKE

First Published in July 2022

ISBN: 978-93-5628-434-0

BLUEROSE PUBLISHERS
www.BlueRoseONE.com
info@bluerosepublishers.com
+91 8882 898 898

Cover Design:
Aman Sharma

Typographic Design:
Sachvesh

Distributed by: BlueRose, Amazon, Flipkart

Author Description

Rohit Jetke is a person who comes from the community of Yerwada, Pune. He completed his graduation in business management and international business, but loves to work in a role of an educator and social worker. He recently joined Teach for India as a teacher and also as a Chairman of The Umang Foundation, an organization that works for the education sector of India. Rohit has experienced many ups and downs in his life, which he says is important for every individual to understand the value of life. He loves talking and interacting with people around him and exploring himself in things that give him happiness.

He has a dream of starting chains of community centers in slums with an intention that whatever he faced in his life he doesn't want anyone else to face and wants to be there for people goes through the same as he went on his journey. Furthermore, he has an artistic view and enjoys getting involved in theaters and leadership opportunities. When Rohit was in school he was a very aggressive person, but with time he changed in aggression into productive things.

"Life is full of ups and downs for everyone, it never comes perfect for anyone. If you have the power to make a change do it and if you cannot make a change or take a step to change what you see is wrong then you are not entitled to complain about it as well".

Rohit Jetke

Acknowledgments

Many people made a great impact in my life some of them are part of the book and have been mentioned but apart from them, there were many more background heroes of my life. I am truly grateful that you all are part of my life and dedicate this book to you all. Mostly I would like to thank my Mother, Father, Aunty, and Grandmother for giving me the best lessons in life, and it was never possible without them. I would also like to thank my teachers Mr. Amar Pol, Mr. Ulhas Kagde, and my school principal Shalini Sachdev for molding me to become the person I am today. Furthermore, I would like to dedicate this book to Pratiksha Dhotre for believing in me and motivating me every time to write whenever I was down and out. Furthermore, my friends who helped me by giving me feedback whenever I wanted and helped me to improve the book and got my best version for this whole process.

Thank you, people, this is not just my hard work, but this is our hard work altogether.

Thank you and love you all.

Table of Contents

The Mistakes that made me...

Rohit Jetke

Chapter 1

Self-Loved Boy

A short but beautiful journey of love, responsibility, dreams, and hard work. In the small city of Pune, Maharashtra lived Sameer. He was a very creative person who always wanted to help and found that helping people is the only thing that gives him happiness. He was himself a mixed bag of emotions and experiences and loved exploring himself. He always wanted to create something big and wanted to be a self-made man and one-day touch the sky and go beyond the moon, where he will become a role model and people will learn from his story. He was a young boy from a middle-class family with a lot of things on his plate. Born in a family of five where his father was the sole bread-earner living was a challenge but having larger-than-life goals made it feel easier to him. The belief that one day his creation would make him the most powerful person because he believed in himself always gave him strength. His childhood was like a rainbow built of all his varied learnings. The school he went to was like a playground for him where he used to create mischief while teachers would complain "Ahhhh.... Sameer how many times are you going to fall in trouble!" He chose not to care and used to inconvenience people. He loved to be in a happy environment, around happy people, and spread smiles. The teachers were upset and worried a lot about Sameer's future, but he never did so because he believed in his own capacity to find happiness.

Being a teenager brought a rollercoaster of twists and turns in life due to the so-called hormonal changes where attractions were built. He found fascination in topics like sex, ended up developing his first crush at school, committing the first pathetic mistake of your life, and so on. In this phase of his life, Sameer found himself hanging out with friends, loved being a backbencher, and was fascinated and attracted to girls; he wanted to have a girlfriend not because he wanted to, but to prove his dignity before the boys he was surrounded by, and to say "Boys, I have a girlfriend" was a way of getting attention at school, and I am confident this is quite natural and this happens with every boy and girl in school... but trust me the school relationships and crush are something extraordinary. No commitments, no responsibilities, no strong bonds, no seriousness, just pure attraction and pure emotion of love.

Sameer was a boy who lived in a two-room house. His dwelling was a part of a chawl which was filled with a variety of people who would fight today but talk and crack jokes with one other tomorrow. He always saw love, fights, brotherhood, and a bond between them. Living in a chawl also showed him problems like alcoholism, domestic violence against women for money, bullying, child abuse, murders, drugs, and gang wars. It was hard to see that many people who used to play with Sameer ended their careers by joining gangs in a series of wrong decisions. Sameer's father owned an alcohol shop. They sold alcohol for their survival.

Sameer's father lost his parents at a very young age. Having the responsibility of two brothers on his shoulders was a tough circumstance, with many difficult decisions to make. For the better future and survival of his brothers and at all of 14 years of age, his father decided to work. At that point of time, he didn't think what was right, he only saw one thing, that his brothers were hungry, and crying. In the 1980s his father worked day and night at an alcohol shop and earned 20 Rs out of which he used to spend 10 Rs on food and spent 10 Rs on household activities. His father never knew that he was going to jump into something muddy, from which he will not able to come back. After working for 2 years, he had his first police complaint registered against him.

After a few years, Sameer's father got married to his mother and from there, things began to change for the good. It's true when they say that a woman has supernatural powers, bringing life to a house that does not have happiness at all. Sameer's mom was such a woman who had a vision for development and wanted to see the family grow for their children. Sameer's mom and dad took the responsibilities of the house and in 1997 Sameer won a race competing with millions of sperms and saw the world for the first time. They were slowly marching for success, as his parents believe that whatever they did will be for the children they had. The things they didn't get in their lives they will make sure that their children get it. They thought, we will teach our children to dream, and we will help them achieve it. As it is rightly said, SURVIVAL OF THE FITTEST.

Chapter 2

Everything for the first time

It was time for Sameer to graduate from the school and step into a challenging world that was full of competition, where the unique person gets opportunities and his/her dreams come true. This is a bitter truth of the society that they judge, judge people for their ability and demotivate people who are not good at the thing they are doing. Sameer growing from 8th standard started seeing this around. He was never into studies but loved to express himself through colors, art, drama, and stuff. Everything started with the family, and they were the first ones to criticize him. “Are you crazy” “what the hell are you doing” “Sameer you are the eldest in the house, you have responsibilities” “idiot go study” and “focus on your grades” these statements were the first strike on young Sameer and this was the time he started to think for the first time about his life and career. He graduated 8th standard with satisfactory marks but was proud that he has a dream to do something big, didn’t know what to do but wanted to do something big. Sameer started his new life at 9th standard, with this promotion of grades he was also promoted from childhood to teenage. 9th was challenging because after this was the last step which was 10th where he had to score for a good college and get a great career.

Every day was similar to Sameer, everything happened for the first time. Teenager Sameer saw his mom being beaten up by his dad for the first time, saw his dad spoil his health by drinking every day, saw his mom leave the house for the first time and saw money can also be a problem to survive for the first time. It was time for him to focus and get serious. He started taking things seriously and started to prepare for his boards for the 10th. Before boards, he had his prelims as a challenge in front of him. He gave it a shot and ended up scoring 37%. It was a bright Monday morning and the school was holding an open day to discuss the scores and grades with parents. "Sameer, come here with your parents" Sameer stood up with a notorious smile on his face and went to the class teacher will full confidence. Standing with his mom in front of a teacher is always a challenge, and the fear of getting scolded is something else. The teacher stood up and spoke to Sameer's mom having an angry look on his face "Ma'am sorry to say, but this boy is wasting your time and school resources, this boy is a waste and will not do anything in his life. Please talk to him and get things sorted, I am very confident that this boy will not clear his 10th." This was the first time when Sameer saw his mom getting insulted and crying because of him. They came home and Sameer's mom just said one thing to him "Boy I had a vision for you that you will get me a better life, but today you proved me wrong" saying this his mom left and Sameer went into deep thought about what should I do. That night Sameer did not sleep and was looking in a mirror and asking the same question to himself what should I do? The next morning brought sun rays of hope to him. Having one statement in his heart "I am going to prove myself" he got ready and went to school with hope. Looking at Sameer for a week with this serious attitude for the first time made teachers believe that yes, he is serious now, and he will do it. It was the last day at school when he said goodbye to his teachers, his friends, and everyone and promised himself that he will grow one day and prove to people that they were wrong and judging him for his ability was wrong. He started studying, whenever he studied upstairs, below his parents were fighting every day, the thought was clear what to be done the only thing that was going on his mind was the score, marks, grade, future nothing else. He appeared for his 10th examination and with his hard work cleared his exams with 75% a change from 37% to 75% made people think it was wrong that we judged his ability. That was the first time when Sameer proved to someone that if he decides he can achieve it and from there he decided to take things seriously to make himself a role model tomorrow.

Sameer not only left school but that day on the goodbye list he had a person, a person who was with him every time, that person who was part of the mischief that was created by Sameer, that person who wiped his tears and was like a family to talk to. He was Akash. This is the first time he realized how it felt to leave a person with whom you have the best memories, when he said you are my brother and will never leave your hand, but it happened didn't know when he will see Akash again, didn't know whenever Sameer will cry, will Akash be there? But it happened. This was the first time Sameer was alone on his journey, the first time when Sameer was seeing someone leave, and the first time when Sameer was upset because someone close to him will not be together. This phase of his life taught him that when something happens for the first time take the experience, learn from it and jump into the bucket of risk when you have nothing to lose that time every first time will be the first experience of life and this will last forever...

Chapter 3

Dreams, Hope and Magic

Dreams are something that gives you hope to do something and achieve it, and ultimately, it fills your life with magic. If you don't have a dream or a goal in life you are a complete zero, but if you have a dream, and you are passionate about it, it becomes the reason to live. After graduating from school, Sameer every day woke up with the same and was finding a reason to live, "what dream should I have" and "what career should I choose?" "What do I like to do" his mind was filled with such questions. I was good at drama, so can I become an actor? I am good at cricket, can I become a cricketer? I am good at art can I become an artist, his mind was filled with these questions as well. He wanted answers, he wanted clarity. The next day, he went to his advisor at school and started a discussion about what he should do. After a discussion for a long hour, he got clarity, and he decided that he is good at arts and is creative, so he decided to go for interior design. The interior design course was expensive, and his family conditions were not so good that they could afford Sameer to go to a college where the admission fees were, 25000rs. The goal he had was astonishing; the career he was trying to look at was wonderful, but the road was filled with stones that he had to overcome. His family was worried as to where to get the money from, he was worried about will I be able to do it? That very moment, a boy from his locality called him. He offered him a job for a month's worth, 10000rs, he was going to get married and wanted a replacement for his place at work. Sameer had no option but to say yes if he wanted to study interior design. He said yes and that was the first job of his life. He started working as a pantry boy in an office

Sameer joined the office, the first day was hard as it was his first job, and he was still struggling to survive in that world. Getting tiffin boxes for the employees, getting their coffee or tea, filling their water bottles, cleaning the tables, washing cups and soccer in the pantry, getting photocopies of documents, and delivering cheques were part of the job which he did every day. It was tough for him as he had never done that kind of job. I am well-educated, completed my 10th from an English medium school, I speak much more fluent English than the employees, I am super talented.... Still, do I deserve to be here and do this job? Sameer used to go in the pantry, spend some time in the washroom, and used to cry a lot for this. Doing this, he spent one month over there, and it was the time for Sameer to leave. But before leaving he had won hearts over there with his skills and people were happy to see a hardworking boy like Sameer. "Sameer come here?" a voice came from the boss cabin. "Yes sir, may I come in," asked Sameer with curiosity on his face. "Take this cheque this is your first salary boy, and all the best for your future" Sameer took the cheque and was looking at it as if it was ruby. He had tears in his eyes, a smile on his face, and replied "thank you, sir, this means a lot. This is not just money for me, this is my ticket to start my career" he met everyone and waved his hand for the last time saying goodbye. He took his bag and left walking through the road and he was just looking at the cheque he received for a month of 10000rs. This was his first salary, the first time he earned for the family and himself. He was the proudest person on the planet that day. He reached home and hugged his mom and said "mom, take this. This is the first salary of your boy. I am proud to say that I am a responsible grown-up today" his mom looked at him as a responsible adult for the first time and proudly went into the neighbors and showed the cheque to everyone with a proud smile on her face. Neighbors came home and congratulated Sameer on his first achievement and gave their son an example of Sameer "learn from him, see he is of your age, but today he is so capable and look at you" that was the first proud day for him because he did many unbelievable things in one day. Earned his first salary, made his mom feel that he is a grown-up now, the first step for him to become a role model and example for the neighbors, and took the first step toward his dream

Before going to bed he went to the mirror and looked at his reflection for 5 minutes. And started talking to the reflection. The feeling was magical, and he said:

Some obstacles were in the pathway,

some feelings pulled me away,

there were times when I had a lot to say,

but through all this, I found my way. I made my way

It is just a matter of time because if the efforts you put in are coming from your heart then at the end of the day it is all worth it......

Chapter 4

The Challenging World

"Sameer, Sameer...... get up good morning" a voice came into the ear and the beautiful dream came to an end. It was a new morning, Sameer woke up with hope and a smile which made his day. He was clear about what he wanted to do, his vision had clarity, and now he knew answers to the what, why, how, and when questions that used to come to his mind every day. He woke up, got ready took his documents, and went to the college for enrolling himself in the course of interior design that he wanted to do. The college was a brand-new place to go after the school, it was similar to a school there to Sameer was going to learn, teachers were there, and students were there, but the environment was entirely different as over there he was going to explore himself in the brand-new world with brand-new people. In college, Sameer had to show the world that he has something so that others will get attracted to him. He saw the environment for the first time, got scared hesitated a bit, "excuse me can you tell me where is the admission process going on?" he asked hesitatingly to the receptionist. "Go up and take the first right" answered the receptionist. He went upstairs with such fear in his mind as if he is going to the border for a war. He found the office and opened the principal's office door. "May I come in, sir?" "Yes boy come in, please grab a seat and tell me how I can help you" He was in relief seeing the kind gesture of the principal. Sameer took a step ahead and asked "Sir I wanted to join the interior designing course and wanted information about it. Can you please help me with the information?" "Sure why not. Can I have your documents, please?" Principal replied. Sameer handed over his mark sheets and certificates to the principal. The principal had a smile on his face and as he turned the pages of the files, the smile increased and became wider. He was delighted to see that such a talented boy wants admission to his college for such a creative course, he gave the file back to Sameer and just said one simple line “I am pleased to have a boy like you be part of my college. You should go ahead and do this course. You will be a role model one day, Sameer”. These statements were new for Sameer he was never used to hearing these kind of words all he ever heard was stupid, idiot, dumb. He was happy he went to the reception filled out the enrollment form and gave that cheque to the cash counter and got his ID card. Sameer was happy, he was feeling like an adult and a grown-up for the first time today. After the college admission, he was just looking at that college, he took a walk on the college premises. Life was something else there, people, students, the environment was something else it was like a free atmosphere, it was similar to what he saw in movies. Looking at that college, taking the surrounding walk he started to walk towards the bus stop, it was 5 pm, and he wasn't aware that time passed so quickly he took a walk towards the bus stop. While walking on the road, he found that the bus stop was 45 minutes away from the college. The routine started, it was never easy to follow it every day, to get exhausted in college, and then take a walk back for 45 minutes to the bus stop. Every morning and afternoon he did the same, in the morning get out of the bus walked to the college for 45 minutes, studied and in the afternoon in the hot sun walk back to the bus stop and then with a hungry stomach wait there for the bus. From college his house was 15 km away, Every day it took 2 hours for him to reach home. And he did this every day. He used to run home as if he was hungry for ages, after coming home he used to eat and use to be so tired that he straightway after eating used to sleep. College was astonishing he met new people, made new friends, and also was enjoying every day of his life to the fullest.

Going to college and shifting his momentum from school to college was a colossal step in his life, and he also experienced the changes, but it was important, this change was important for him to grow, grow as an adult, and the world was challenging, but it was important to survive, he learned one thing from the experience of college that this is a competitive world if you are different you will survive here, no one will spoon-feed you in college like there used to be in school, no one would ask you what's wrong, you need to be strong and attract people towards you then only college is a life that you will cherish throughout your life or else you will regret rest of your life that you had time, that time if you had done it, the days would have been much more different and worth remembering. Every day was a challenge but when you tell yourself that you are a grown-up, that time you need to make these changes and take this risk as a champion.

Chapter 5

Community Centre

When living in a chaawl it is very difficult to survive in such an environment where people fight daily, alcohol is something because of which arguments happen in every house daily, drugs are available easily, bullying and molestation are seen every day, and gang war and murders are something that happens occasionally. But what is more difficult is to see these things in front of your eyes. Sameer was a socially challenging person, when he used to see these things he used to think every day about changing these things for the community he is living for but still, he was unable to do anything, he was unable to find an answer to the question. In the school where Sameer used to go, it was always taught to stand against wrong deeds and things, and do what is right, no matter how difficult the pathway is then.

In Sameer's school days he had his Marathi teacher his name was Mr. Amar, he was a Marathi subject teacher by profession but was a social worker as well. He was a very humble person; he was like a friend to his students. Sameer also saw a friend in him, and slowly he started sharing his problem and asked for solutions from him. Doing this their bond became more strong, with this Mr. Amar, also introduced Sameer to a thing he used to do after school that was something huge for Sameer at this age to see. It was a community center that he used to run in a slum community, It was free of cost community center with just one objective that was to help, and guide the community children towards success. This community center was known for providing these children with a voice but also giving them a second chance which their parents didn't give them. It was something amazing to see what he was doing. Sameer started visiting the center and learned numerous things and the great value of giving back to society from there.

Once Mr. Amar had organized a summer camp for the students of his center, he also invited Sameer to be part of it. Sameer was very happy and said yes to it, Sameer packed his bag and went to the summer camp. It was so beautiful to see a village after ages, with so many people of his age group. They used to cook their food, attend sessions every day, sing prayers together, and do everything on their own. That village was a very peaceful place to be, it was away from the polluted air of the city, fresh breeze used to touch the faces every day, they used to take a bath at the river used to climb the tree to get tamarinds it was a perfect childhood feeling.

Once there was a session in the summer camp on the social responsibility of an individual. The professor was a social worker and started his presentation with some stories and photographs of the situation. The situations were those which Sameer saw every day in his community. He was super amazed to see this but was quietly listening to everything that the professor was talking about, the professor not only told about the problem but was also talking about how you at this age you can stand up for the community you are living in, that very moment Sameer's attention went to Mr. Amar, that time he asked himself one question "if he can do it why can't I?" "the community center that he is running in his community is a need in my community as well? Why can't I start it?" he went to Mr. Amar and spoke his heart out told him that he also want to start something like this. Mr. Amar was happy that he want to do it but with that, he also told him that all the things might happen with it, he also told him that if he starts something like this there won't be a looking back. Sameer asked for time to think as it was a huge commitment to make at the end of the day it was about the future, the future of children who will be coming to the community center every day.

It was the last day of the summer camp, he left for home with the thought of doing the project because Mr. Amar was right there was no looking back. He went back home. Life was back to normal, the next day he heard a 15 years old boy was beaten up by his family as they caught him selling drugs. One thing changed in Sameer after coming back from the summer camp, that was his perspective of looking at society, that moment seeing that boy being beaten up made him realize that this is the root of all the problems in India. He was studying in an environment where education had value, where he was taught to be a good human being, where he was taught that whatever we take from nature it asks us back and we need to give back to society as well. At that time it was important to get these children back on track. He shared this with Mr. Amar and he suggested Sameer to start a branch of his community center in Sameer's locality. A hope came into the mind of Sameer and he started working on it. He was so passionate about the project that within a week he arranged all the things right from arranging the space, to finding children he did everything. At that time funds and money were a problem, but Sameer overcame it and invested from his pocket money. He started the community center with 10 rs, and he kept the doors open, first, there were only 5 students who came to the center but the next day number increased and went to 15, and within 3 weeks the project was so successful that 300 students came to the center. This showed Sameer how important this community center was in his locality. In the center, he focused on academics but more importantly, he focused on personality development. He had a vision that school is providing education but through his community center, he provided the knowledge which is important to live in the real world that is values.

Days were going well, people were bullying, as well as some boys of the society also used to tease girls while coming to the center, throw stones at the center, and abused children to not go to the center, but it didn't stop. One day, a boy threw a stone at Diksha. She was a 4th standard girl from the center, it hit her so badly that she was bleeding. Sameer was scared and decided not to continue and risk the student's life, but the next day Diksha with a bandage on her forehead came to Sameer's house and said to Sameer "it's time to go to the center Dada, why are you not ready, come on let's go" that was the moment Sameer realized that his efforts were going in the right direction and his vision one day will come into existence. He started again. After a few months, Sameer had to shut the community center as his mom was hospitalized for stomach surgery. But he knew he will come back soon, when didn't know but will come back soon. As he was the only boy in the family he had to support the family as well and at that time he had a choice he chose family because it was important.

From this Sameer understood one thing, when it comes to family sometimes we have to make hard choices, and when this situation comes it is difficult to decide he also understood this was just the beginning many more situations like these were on the way for him.

Chapter 6

Umang

The community center stopped, and it was bothering Sameer every day. Umang is a powerful word that brings hope to everyone's life, this word also enlightened Sameer. This was not just a simple word for Sameer, but it was a reason to live. It is true when you say dreams are not those which come when you sleep, dreams are those which don't let you sleep, Umang was such a dream for him. He was creative, he had leadership qualities, and he had an ability for problem-solving, but what is the use of it if you don't utilize these skills of yours in the right direction and change your life with it. These values, these ethics are simply waste if you cannot utilize them to do something big.

One day sitting at the bus stop he looked at an artist who was a boy of around 19 years, he was playing a guitar own road, Sameer was with his friends at the bus stop, his friends were making fun of that boy but Sameer was looking at that boy as if it was himself, that boy was playing guitar beautifully, he attracted people to the bus stop and people were amazed to see that boy play that guitar, the melody was mesmerizing, and he stopped. People were clapping continuously and started clicking pictures with him. He was not a celebrity; he was not a professional, still why people made him one? This question came to Sameer's mind. After that boy stopped playing Sameer went to him and asked him who was he, that boy told him that he never does these performances for money, he does this because he wants people to know his talent, he does this because he doesn't have a platform or a medium to perform, he does this to improve because he was rejected by some people and was notified that he cannot do it because he doesn't have enough skills that he will be an ideal.

Talent is a very heavy word; it has deep meaning, but what everyone understands from that is UNIQUENESS. If you have a talent that no one has then you are unique, that means you are talented. Listening to that boy was a strike for Sameer's mind. Is this the real world? When Sameer asked himself this question, one incident from his past came in front of him. When Sameer was in school he always loved to be on the stage, be a hero of stage and drama, and loved to attract people as an artist, there was a group that came to the school, that group was doing a musical theater and wanted to audition for dancers, actors, and singers for it, Sameer was the first one to register for it, the next day he went to the audition room, he sang a beautiful Bollywood song and got a green light for singing, he went to the next door for a drama audition, he was given a situation to act with different emotions in 30 seconds, he was a filmy guy he acted the maximum emotions and got a green light there as well. When he went to the third room for dance, it was a challenge. It was instructed that you have to copy the steps and do the same looking once, it was very difficult but had to do for the selection. The music started, and he had to perform 10 steps, but performed one step incorrectly and was rejected. He was very upset, went to the choreographer and asked for one more chance to prove but was unable to get it. He can outside, and some of his friends were crying because of this rejection. Sameer that day realized what is the meaning of heartbreak, and rejection, and how does it feels when someone neglects you because you have some skills missing.

When Sameer saw that boy he got an idea, the idea that he was looking all over his life what will be that thing that he will do different which he will do worth remembering for ages not for himself, but for such people who don't have resources. He decided to catch hold of these people who once got a rejection and start a musical theater group of his own. He never knew what will be the future of this group, he never thought that how will he do it, but he knew one single thing that it will happen I will make it happen, he started working on the plan. He knew it was difficult to start this group it was very difficult to find these people, but the hope was pure, and the dream was clear. It was time to decide a name for this group and his theater group.

Looking at the plan felt like hope to many, it felt like it was just sunlight in the darkness for many. It is like a candle for fears in mind. At that very moment, one word came from Sameer's mind, UMANG. And that was the time Umang was born. A revolution started, and he named his theater group UMANG MUSICAL GROUP. A dream was seen that day. He went to his friend the next day in college and discussed this idea, he got everyone and everyone said that this is huge, and you will never be able to do it. Sameer also knew he will not be able to do it but still his vision, and efforts were so strong that these words never demotivated him but filled his heart with countless hopes that this is possible, and that it will happen. That was the time Sameer decided he will do it and this is the dream which will change his life and will help him prove himself to the world to every person that ever said Sameer is a failure.

Chapter 7

D – Day

It is easy to see a dream and tell yourself that this is the dream that I want to do. It is easy to say that I wish to become something in my life, it's easy to say I have a dream or a goal in life but when it comes to execution and working for it, many of us get scared looking at the failure and the pathway before taking the first step. Confidence and motivation break down into pieces, and then people stop working for it. Sameer not only saw a dream but had the power and ability to fulfill it, and that was the reason he was different from others. It is important to see yourself with your dream until the final destination if you can see the picture clearly you will make it, Sameer for the first time saw himself to the finishing line. That day Umang was possible for him even if people criticized him. The dream was ready, the concept was ready, and the plan was almost ready, it was now essential to have a team to work with Sameer in this long run. It was hard to convince someone to work with him for his dream, and most important to convince them to be with him and trust him. It was a hard nut to crack, but it was not impossible.

Sameer made a team by collecting a team of failures and the goal was clear that one day we want to make our musical production and make our theater show and one day perform on the world's biggest stage that is Wembley Stadium, London. Wembley was the dream he was fascinated with, he was crazy about it as it was the first love of his life, his room was filled with posters of Wembley, and the walls were decorated with the concept, with the charts everywhere which had a title of ROAD TO WEMBLEY. He did it every day and researched how to go there. Every day he used to gather information and improvise it and change plans. Every day he used to think something is missing but after doing this for 6 long months of research the plan was ready to start. He started making advertisements for hiring, started making posters, and started working on it. The concept was spectacular, but everything needs time so that people can trust it.

Sameer went to some people in the chaawl he lived but no one gave a positive response but laughed saying sorry boss we are not made for this, went to his college friends and asked them to join in, but they also said the same thing. The team was important without the team it would not be possible to achieve the goal. The next day he was thinking about a solution for this and that day he got a call from his sister's school and the principal asked his parents to come to the school. Sameer's parents were not around, so he went himself to see what was the problem. When he entered the office at that time, the principal was standing with his sister's report card with red marks on it. Her principal was very upset, looking at the constant zero on her report card. Sameer entered the room and started talking to the principal. It was humiliating to see this but at the same time, it was necessary because it was his responsibility. After the conversation, Sameer left with his sister from the office, passing by a classroom he saw a group of students and teachers practicing a drama which was a street play, which they were doing. He went back to the principal and asked the principal what this drama was all about. The principal replied, saying it was a preparation act that is being practiced for the school's annual function. He was amazed to see that finally, he saw a perfect group of people to join his team and be part of Umang.

He started having a conversation with the principal about Umang and his plan and told her everything that he had an idea about. She was so impressed to see a boy like Sameer and was amazed that Riya was his sister. The principal was delighted to be part of this. Sameer asked her out of curiosity, can he have auditions in their school? She was so impressed, that she said yes without giving it a second thought. This time he was very motivated and finally saw the sun in the darkness. He now started to talk to his school friends and got 3 people to join this movement. Slowly and steadily the army was forming, and now it was time to go to the school to take the auditions.

Sameer saw more than 30 people for the auditions, and it was the first time he felt so responsible that people liked the idea and the concept so much that they came here to be part of the group, it was the first time he was talking to so many people together, it was the first time when he was going to take auditions. It was a big day, D –DAY for him because today he was not an ordinary boy, today he was a leader. A leader who was going to guide artists and take them to Wembley.

He went to the audition room and people started entering one by one. His friends and Sameer started to take the auditions. The artists were remarkable, the panelist and Sameer did not say no to anyone because he believed that even if the person has a lack of skills still if the will is strong then Umang Musical is the perfect place for them. The performances were astonishing one by one the performances were just mesmerizing, dancing after that act, after that singing. No one was perfect at anything, but it was important to give them a chance and Sameer was so happy because he saw that spark on their face and saw the honesty of these people who were performing that was the reason Sameer selected everyone. After the hard work of 6 hours, the wait was over, and now he had a team. Yesterday he was alone and today there were 30 people with him to make it happen. That day was the D DAY because today Sameer become a leader, today he was responsible for 30 people now he cannot take a step behind, and he had to do it with these people now to not only prove themselves but also to prove every single person who was there in his team. The team was filled with countless stories within the group. There was a person who had parents who were constantly fighting over money problems, there was a girl who was being forced by her family to get married, there was a girl who had dyslexia and dysgraphia, there was a dwarf boy, there was a girl who was unable to speak properly. But still, these people were together because they believed in one word together, that is CHANGE. They were all together to create and change and tell the world that even if the days are not going your way if things are not working well trust yourself that one day it will be there, D – DAY that day you will create your own life with your hands.

into their fa[illegible] and saw the h[illegible]ry of these people [illegible] [illegible] that [illegible] the reason [illegible] [illegible] figures [illegible] was over [illegible] that [illegible] sorely [illegible] and today, them [illegible] to the [illegible] happen[illegible] and was [illegible] became [illegible] day [illegible] [illegible] the [illegible] cut [illegible] [illegible]

Chapter 8

The Journey

Life changed like a spinning wheel. It was like yesterday Sameer was all alone but today he was a leader of a group, many people were looking upon him that this person will change our life, that this boy will take us there where we belong where people will admire us not criticize us, where people will appreciate our talent and not judge us for the lack of skills we have. That day Sameer realized one thing it is not easy to become a leader. Road to Wembley was very difficult as it is always said that big dreams and thoughts don't come without big challenges. It was very difficult to figure out what should be done, Sameer and his team didn't know how it will happen but they just knew one thing we need to do this to prove to people that yes even if we lack at skills but still our voices matter, we still exist.

After a lot of research and talking to many people it was very important for Sameer to understand the team and more importantly, it was necessary to make his team confident that it is possible. Sameer decided to take small steps and divided his road to Wembley into small milestones. He started with street plays and flash mobs on the streets of Pune. They didn't have a place to practice so went to a nearby hilltop and started practicing over there. Boys use to bully and tease girls and the team, they use to crack jokes and pass comments on the physical appearance of girls. It was very hard to digest these things but we let them go and still practiced. The script was made, roles and characters for the street play were assigned dialogues were set. After practicing for a week it was time to perform. The first meeting was worth remembering "this is your first time to perform, this is your first step to prove, don't worry about the result even if you fail today I will always be proud of you all. In this journey, the learning is more important for me rather than the performance. So just go and give your best shot to the world as if there is no second chance." These were the first words to the team by Sameer as a leader. They didn't have money so they contributed from their pocket money and went to the location at MG Road circle. It was a crowded place. They hugged each other and went to perform. People got attracted by sudden singing and people gathered to see the street play. The confidence was boosted by the first round of applause by the crowd. The team was so good that people taught it was happening for real. It was a success. Sameer was not part of the play but was having a donation box in his hand and was moving within the crowd for money. After the play, the team was in tears they didn't know it happened and they were fully confident this time. From the first play, they got 500rs as donations. They were starving since morning but still didn't feel hungry and wanted to do more plays and went to the next market nearby and did two plays. A newspaper team of Times of India was passing by and saw them perform. They waited and after the play, the reporter started talking to them. They were very impressed. They wanted to interview the team on their journey and called them for an interview at their office the next day.

They went to their office the next day, and everyone was nervous to see this happening, so they did the photoshoot and interviewed the group for the journey. After 2 hours the team left the office with sparkling smiles on their faces. After two days the article was written with their photograph. The title of the article was UMANG - PUNES UPCOMING REVOLUTION. This was their first strike at their parents, the world, their friends, and everyone who thought they cannot do anything. On the day the article was published, people started to call and started to congratulate them, Sameer and the team met that day and celebrated they laughed, smiled, and cried but at the end of the day, they knew it started hugely. They started to get opportunities and calls to perform street plays, and also performed a flash mob at the airport on the 15th of August. After reading the articles a recognized company AIRTEL also wanted Umang Musical to work with them for marketing.

It was just a matter of time that yesterday Umang was just a name and today it was a revolution. It just happened because they believed in the idea they were working for, they believed in the thought and they believed in change all together.

Chapter 9

The Greatest Show on Earth

After the journey started small opportunities were coming on the way. People started recognizing them, and the name they were working for was getting popular day by day. One fine morning one of the members of Umang called Sameer and said "bhaiya, my school is participating in a street play competition and they want our help to set up the play, could you help them? He said, "sure we will help them." The next day Sameer went to the school and started teaching and helping the children. It was a hard nut to crack as these children were very notorious and mischievous. These children were seen in all the mischief that was happening in school and the school wanted these children to invest their time into something productive.

So, here he was with this team of 15 artists and started working with them. It was difficult to bring these children to work with the same power and vision he was thinking in his mind but one thing that brought these children together was the power of love and brotherhood. He started working with them as their elder brother and after hard work for 2 weeks they were ready to perform. The team was weak for the competition and the other teams had experts in theatres with them. But they were not scared or afraid as they had nothing to lose because they didn't have the pressure of losing or the stress of winning it was just one thing in mind to enjoy what they were doing. They performed and within 10 strong teams, won the first prize that very moment he realized that he was becoming a good leader and also a good theatre artist. They got awards, certificates, medals, and appreciation but with that Sameer was waiting for something else to be announced that the winning team will get a chance to go to Mumbai and perform the play at a conference. This was a turning point not only for the kids but Umang as well.

Everyone was excited and happy and started marching towards the Mumbai show. The atmosphere was very different. Lots of educators, social workers, etc. were there for the event he felt like these people are super successful and I am like a small creature in front of them, but he knew he was not just an ordinary person he was a leader as he was running such a revolutionary movement for many children and youth. When they reached the conference Sameer saw a person. She was a role model he admired, a person Sameer wanted to be like, he just heard stories about her success but never got a chance to talk to her. She was Shaheen Didi CEO of Teach for India. She was attending a session and sitting there with a cup of coffee in her hand. Sameer was super nervous to go there and talk to her but gathered some confidence and went to have a word with her. "Hello didi" he said in a small voice with fear, but her next sentence vanished Sameer's fear altogether. "Hi, how are you? come sit, did you attend the sessions?" she said with a huge smile on her face as if she is welcoming him to talk to her. "Yes, I did didi the sessions were really good and informative. I wanted to talk to you about Umang." Sameer said. "Umang I already know about it I have heard about it." This sentence from such a big personality that she knows Umang was an achievement. Sameer explained everything about Wembley. She was super excited about the idea and without thinking a lot she offered Sameer an opportunity to work with her and do THE GREATEST SHOW ON EARTH. It was a musical depicting the education sector in a form of a circus. He said yes and accepted her offer. Mumbai trip was a turning point as he said because he was taking back something with him from there. Maybe the biggest opportunity which will add more value to the organization. When he came back to Pune they met again and discussed how will they do it and the journey began. After practicing for 6 months, the musical was ready. The journey was full of experiences where they learned a lot of things, met new people, understood the team more clearly, learned lots of values, argued a lot, smiled a lot, and most importantly created the best bonds with each other. Umang got its first opportunity to perform at the Royal Opera House, Mumbai. It was an auditorium where actors use to perform but they were also on that stage now. After the three words of lights, camera, and action curtains were up and in front of them people were cheering them, clapping for them, it felt like the hard work paid off because, in that crowd, their parents were also there.

After the show, people started to take pictures with them it felt like they were brand new celebrities. Sameer still gets goosebumps remembering that day because it was magical, still feels like it was a beautiful dream that happened that night. After the Mumbai show, they also got an opportunity to perform in Mumbai, Pune, and Delhi. They were growing very fast. The sky was the limit for Umang and today they were unstoppable. This was not a one-day gift they got but this was the gift they earned and saw the word impossible from their perspective as I'm possible and they made it, created it the way they wanted it to look from their hard work.

Chapter 10

Tough Choice

Everything was going his way, but this was just his passion. It was hard to digest that Sameer was in such a situation that his parents wanted him to take responsibility for the house and start earning and focusing on his higher education. After completing his diploma in interior designing Sameer was clear that he wanted to do a degree in interior design and decoration. He started searching for colleges. Fees were high so high that he was not able to afford it as it was a 6-digit number. Still, he gave it a try and went to different colleges with his parents. The degree program sounded interesting but he could see the question on his mom's face how will she arrange the money? They dropped that college.

Next week Sameer went with his dad to another college. Looking at his skills college agreed to not only give them a discount on the fees but also offered him to work at the college so that they can manage the amount of the fees from the salary. It was a great offer that they presented and without thinking a lot he and his father said yes. His parents took a loan of 40000rs and paid his first installment and Sameer got enrolled. He started going to college as well and started attending lectures. It was amazing learning something different rather than solving math equations in commerce, doing experiments in science, and learning theory in arts and engineering. Every day Sameer went to college with the hope that today he will do something new. He also started working there after college. The routine was set that in the morning he will do his lecture and in the afternoon till evening will work.

The work which was given to him was handling inquiries and converting leads to admission. Sameer enjoyed talking to new people and convincing them, he was good at it though so it was not difficult at all. For a month everything was going well. Until one evening he got an inquiry, he called the number. It was a girl. He started talking to her and slowly she told him how badly she wanted to do the fashion design course. She was very much interested in the course. She told him about her family as well and told him that she was a single parent and there were lots of family problems in her family, Pune was new for her and no one was there in Pune who could help her.

Her story touched him and he told her that she could go for it not only officially but he could help her on a personal level as well to help her find a PG and help her settle down. She was grateful for these words from Sameer and agreed to get the admission. They exchanged numbers and Sameer started talking to her about her requirements. They talked for around a week and all of a sudden he got a call from his manager and asked to meet her in the office. He was confused by her tone and was thinking about what exactly happened he went to the cabin and she looked at him with doubt and said "I told you not to help anyone personally, it could have been a fake call as well" he didn't know what she was talking about in the beginning but then she should him an email which was sent to all the managers and head office with all the screenshots of the conversation. That girl deleted all her messages she did and made up a situation in which Sameer was shown guilty. She had all the proofs so everyone listened to her and he was not heard and the college declared him guilty. They asked him to resign from the job and just study. Sameer was shocked and felt embarrassed, he left from there and went to his friend's house because what should I tell my mom? Why did they remove me? These questions were making him crazy. He went to his friend and cried a lot and came home at night. He gained some confidence and told his mom that I don't want to do the job because it is affecting his studies but didn't tell her the truth.

An argument started in his house with it. Everyone started shouting and blaming him. It was really hard for him to bear it. He was feeling so guilty that he decided to harm himself but stopped and started thing about what was next, what should I do. His mom didn't speak to him for days. He use to go to college and straight away come home. As he was still to pay his next installment it was difficult to arrange money and his family was also getting affected by it. Everyone in college was looking at him with a doubtful eye as if they were not safe when he was around. Every day was humiliating and after his limit of handling everything that was happening was over he decided to drop off out of college and left the college. After that as well things didn't change but rather became worse for him. He was a dropout now and need to do something to keep his life going. Sameer started working as a food delivery boy. For 6 months he did it.

Every day getting up, and drove in the hot sun, having back pains still he did it so that he can raise money for his next degree admission next year. The job was sometimes humiliating because people use to think he was unhealthy, dirty as he was sweating, and insulted him sometimes but they didn't know that there was a reason to do it. At that time he realized life is unfair for many people who does this kind of job. And with that, he also learned that helping people blinding can get you in trouble. This time helping a person didn't only cost him his job but also harmed his career and he had to leave a degree that he wished and dreamed to do. It was a lesson for him for life and this experience showed him the real world and the real people around him.

Chapter 11

Meera

Teenage is an age where goals, dreams, and careers are given more priority but with that one more thing comes on the plate which we don't plan that is love. A beautiful feeling that you attract to. At this age, we start looking at the opposite gender differently. It feels like every day comes with a burst of sunshine, every breeze feels fresh and touches your face romantically, everything has music, your heart pumps faster than usual and you feel like a Bollywood hero when you look at the person, you have a crush on. There is also such a girl in Sameer's life. She is Meera.

In his teenage Sameer also went into a relationship with Neha, it was a serious relationship he had with her. They spent a lot of time together and also planned a lot of things for the future, but it never happened she was a very studious girl and also was very ambitious. She had plans for the future that he was never a part of. She applied for a college in the USA and got selected. It still reminds Sameer of the day when she came to him and just said "I am selected for such an opportunity, I am going," he asked her "what about us" and she said, "Sameer I cannot think about us at this moment I have to leave for my career." She left him crying, he cried for a month and felt heartbroken for the first time but no one was there for him at that time.

In this dark pace of his life when Neha did this to him, he got Meera. Sameer never knew Meera had a crush on him when he was all alone she was there to hold his hand and say "don't worry Sameer what happens if Neha is not there, I am here and will always be with you." It was difficult to understand what Meera wanted to say at that time. One day when they were practicing for the greatest show on earth he saw a girl in a black dress. She looked like a fairy. There was bright sunlight on her face, her hairs were flying with the wind, her smile touched his heart, and her eyes were searching him everywhere. In that sunlight, he was trying to see who was this fairy, it was Meera. That very moment he realized that Neha was just an imagination but Meera was the reality he was looking for and don't know what happened that very moment he went to her and hugged her, it felt like home. True love is in front of you but you always run for sparkles around it. Similar happened to Sameer. That very moment he proposed Meera and said "Meera I love you" when he said this there were tears in his eyes, a smile on his face, and some guilty in his eyes that he was not able to recognize that she loves him and he loves her too. On that day he spent some time with her. She had magic in her presence, her presence and love filled his heart with it and it felt like his heart was having one name for the first time it was here.

It was difficult to understand each other because they were in a serious relationship but didn't got time to know each other. It started creating problems between them. Many times they started arguing about silly things but he liked everything that was happening and she was a perfect example of a girl he wanted. She was stubborn, mischievous, romantic, silly, and responsible but she was Sameer's now. She was such a girl who never argued with him about gifts, she understood what his situation is and always said that You are the biggest gift to me. It was still a dream that he got her but slowly when they started to argue it felt like yes this is the reality, not a dream. Everything was normal until that day which never had to come, if that day wouldn't come the bond would have been something else.............

Printed by Libri Plureos GmbH in Hamburg,
Germany